The Corpus Callosum

The Corpus Callosum

Spring 2025

Eric R. Tucker, editor

Corpus Callosum Press LLC
Hastings, Nebraska

Typography and book design by Corpus Callosum Press LLC, Hastings, Nebraska.

Earthrise image on front and back covers by NASA/Bill Anders.

All interior photos of Earth by NASA.

About Earthrise, from nasa.gov: Taken aboard Apollo 8 by Bill Anders, this iconic picture shows Earth peeking out from beyond the lunar surface as the first crewed spacecraft circumnavigated the Moon, with astronauts Anders, Frank Borman, and Jim Lovell aboard.

ISBN-13 979-8-9928127-0-1

National boundaries are not evident when we view the
Earth from space. Fanatical ethnic or religious or national
chauvinisms are a little difficult to maintain when we see
our planet as a fragile blue crescent fading to become an
inconspicuous point of light against the bastion and citadel
of the stars.

Carl Sagan, *Cosmos*

[M]ere critical thinking, without creative and intuitive
insights, without the search for new patterns, is sterile
and doomed. To solve complex problems in changing
circumstances requires the activity of both cerebral
hemispheres: the path to the future lies through the corpus
callosum.

Carl Sagan, *The Dragons of Eden: Speculations on the
Evolution of Human Intelligence*

Contents

Meninges

(protective)(coverings)

01110100 01101000 01100101 01110010 01101101 01101111
01110011 01110000 01101000 01100101 01110010 01100101

Dura Mater

(house of)(bricks)

01101101 01100101 01110011 01101111 01110011 01110000
01101000 01100101 01110010 01100101

Arachnoid

(house of)(sticks)

01110011 01110100 01110010 01100001 01110100 01101111
01110011 01110000 01101000 01100101 01110010 01100101

You have to imagine the moon

is quiet: no kids, no dogs
yet. No corporate headquarters,
no neon, no froyo.

There's a golf ball
but no real course,
no green for any greens,
no water

hazards.
Still,

I imagine walking there,
sitting under a fig tree
to think deep things
like

how,
from this red couch
in my dear living room,
I watch
the earth

slide slow
from a bend in the horizon
smooth

into this sky.

Matt Mason

The Stars Do

The stars do
know my name,
though they haven't called it
for ages.

They watch
for light
in my bedroom window,
dark

as they glide
bright along their bridge
from evening's shore
to dawn.

On some deep night,
good souls,
the light will
wink

and we
will wake
our throats
again

Matt Mason

Pia Mater

(house of)(straw)

01110100 01110010 01101111 01110000 01101111 01110011
01110000 01101000 01100101 01110010 01100101

Cerebral Cortex

(motor, sensory, and)(association)

01101110 01101111 00100000 01100001 01100010 01101111
01110110 01100101 00100000 01101110 01101111 00100000
01100010 01100101 01101100 01101111 01110111

Overview of a dead Earth

In a cave on our moon
on the ever-dark side
near a frigid south pole
lay a sarcophagus of life

Here the cold is so deep
cells may be frozen, yet viable
DNA, RNA, proteins transfixed
as in liquid Nitrogen here

We the keepers put them there
from so many birds and beasts
Flowers, fungi, their embryonic germ,
an arc of the covenant, irretrievable

Held for some wiser race
not prone to our nuclear folly
Statistically improbable but
perhaps safe beyond our grasp

When our biosphere is shorn
to mere microbes, as it began
there's hope of revival, guided
by kinder, gentler minds

Will they know to look here?
Some cypher left on Earth?
Would they want to revive us?
Despoilers, who sought insurance

Not just a pair of each species
Stem cells of at least a hundred
to ensure genetic variety, when
or wherever this ark may land

These are bioengineers:
producers, pollinators,
alchemists, enrichers of soil,
builders of reef and strata

They may have their chance
to reset Earths' life *ex situ* on
a terraformed Mars or undersea
of some icebound Jovian moon

Ironic that we usurpers become
overseers, recreators, Gaian
It's an achievable dream
But please, save no Man

Bill Beachly

Cerebrum

(movement)(temperature)

01100110 00101000 01101111 01110010 00101001 01100101
01110110 01100101 01110010

Frontal Lobe

(voluntary)(movement)

01110111 01100101 00100000 01100011 01101000 01101111
01110011 01100101 00100000 01110100 01101000 01101001
01110011

Night watch

Dark of night
eyelids
roller shades
        get pulled
                slide up
                I am
                        echo
                shadow
                set free
        of its body
all body

afterlife
of unfit
that didn't make
        the cut
                in the whole
                still here
                        in the part
                all those
                hairs pricked
                jaws clenched
        open ears
        don't tend
toward saving
a sleeping
clan
anyone
anymore

all those night-
watchers long
        gone

rising up
when
          all those
          centuries of
                    while
          everyone
          sleeps
vigil-
ant even after
the fire's
died
rising up
when
I raise
          my eyes
                    a vigil
                    for their
                    ancient

                              keep them
                                        this is
                              keep us
                                        how I
                              save them
                                        knew how
                              save us
                                        through skin
                              save me

                    open-
          ing,
listen—

Ali Beheler

Foregrounding

Universe, we were   swallowed
bodies drowning   in plastic
so bright   so clear
so well-defined against   the unseen=
their backgrounds   forgotten

thirsty by sea   forget sea
hungry by sea   forget underneath
blue ball, dark sky   forget sky

vellus limning skin   horizon=
bright line   point of
all attention   vanishing

landing here   not choking
on our wants   not leaching
all our loves   not lasting, we

Universe, we   forgot we
were bodies   were water
drowning   were tree
in all our   destined for
clarity   dust

Ali Beheler

Broca's Area

(speech)(production)

01101110 01101111 00100000 01110111 01101111 01110010
01100100 01110011

Temporal Lobe

(memory)(emotion)

01100011 01101100 01101111 01110011 01100101 00100000
01111001 01101111 01110101 01110010 00100000 01100101
01111001 01100101 01110011

Whose Voice

I think of myself a bundle
        of blotched flesh filled
        with the anguish of existence

someone stares at me I imagine
        with a smile

these beginnings shadowed unknown
        bathed in a baptismal font

a man in robes alcohol breath
        water trickle down my forehead

the anguish of existence trussed
        on a scaffold   of lies

a rocking horse a wire recorder

daddy's eye-openers mommy's rage

hope blows across the prairie
        like a tumbleweed

I read somewhere that every word
        ever said exists in the ether

whose voice would you like to hear
        if you could

Charlie Brice

Parietal Lobe

(sensory)(input)

01110100 01101111 01101111 00100000 01101101 01110101
01100011 01101000 00100000 01110000 01100001 01101001
01101110

Urania's Mirror

When Urania's bell worked, when it came with a
report, she wanted to hear it. She *loved* to hear it, this
bell that was less tone than feeling, rippling along
her spine like water trickling down the throat of a
bone-dry riverbed. Each user's bell was unique so
when things went right, when it came with a report,
Urania's bell was, for her, bold bursts of color by a
window into the unknown, with intimations of both
terror and delight.

But that was when it worked. Because the thing
had just gone off *again*, snapping the girl awake at
5:00 a.m. And now she was sitting up in bed, looking
for a report that she knew would never come, bitter at
the empty promise of a broken bell.

These rings without reports … As a tap nurse,
Urania knew all too well what kind of a problem this
was. Alerts and reports together were what pushed
connections through the general network, across
space and time, each user being their own node.
Yet on rare occasions, especially with cheaper taps,
you'd get a user experiencing rings without reports.
Changes, maybe … but what was the point of it all if
the user could not track or see the results?

This specific glitch had affected Urania's tap a lot
lately, waking her three times last week and twice
the previous night. So she squinted now and tried to
ignore it. She slipped out of bed, naked. She ate her
meal squares so fast she nearly choked, then let the
WC scrub her weary body down for the double at

the clinic. Somewhere in all of this, the song of her broken bell went away.

Whenever Urania felt stressed, she tapped. When she grew bored or anxious, she tapped and although the job at the clinic had come with training that made her better at tapping than most, this hadn't resulted in habits that were any different than anyone else's. She walked down to Dale's for the usual fat cup of coffee, tapping as she waited in a line that was shorter than usual. She then spent the pressurized and silent, eastbound shuttle hurtling through the heavy murk of the city limits to its even darker center, where her clinic was, lost in deep remembering … though, through tapping, this was less reassembly and more revision. *Life*, but lived in four-dimensional space.

Hazy strings, these were, when unassisted: desiccated elements of a trip with her mother twelve years ago, when Urania was only seven, to the Goodlands on the northern California coast. Individual strands, faces and feelings and notions afloat like the loose ends they were, in a pulsating wind. Sometimes touching, yet never seeming to touch the same way twice. But when she centered herself within the tap, she was there again, reliving it. At the beginning of a unified thread of a day and at the end of it, one smooth and twisted loop of all at once.

And with her skill and talent and training, so was the rest, all of it in granular detail: Urania's mother Debbie, the soft and raw blonde who'd died while dreaming a few months later. Uncle Randy from southern Oregon, who'd raised his baby-sister's kid

the best he could after Debbie passed in the night,
and when Urania grew up and ran off to the city,
he stayed behind in that ancient log cabin. His two
buddies from college, too, were there that day on a
beach that was hot and kinetic, the sea breeze soaked
in silk and sweat; graying geneticists who'd adopted,
late, two siblings from out past the catchment because
they'd never been able to conceive on their own.
Their boy Luis, who graduated as an orbital designer
just twenty-four months before dying of stroke
late last year, in the sleeping car of a moon-bound
shuttle. And his little sister Maria, pretty and five …
that small, raised mole on her right wrist. The tap
reminding Urania that this poor little girl had also
died recently, in one of the seedier sections of the
orbiting ring.

Everyone and everything, good or bad, happy
and sad: All right there or more precisely, right *here*,
tendrils of connection stretched before and after
them. Even the rainbow-themed cars of the train that
schussed high above the beach party, tracing out the
border of an ochre cliff that went up and away so
dramatically that it seemed to never stop. The brown
wagon, a single silver scratch on its driver-side door;
a mechanized squirrel, frisky and gray with a puffball
tail, arcing its wet nose at the buzzing train from the
thinning boughs of a western hemlock—

Urania tapped further back.

She dropped into the sunnier part, she sped
forward once again to the moment when the sun
sagged through clouds and fell like a hot stone into
the ocean, pressing the Pacific and everything else

through its billowing screen of orange and blue. Waves that were black and green went brown again, a bruise that turned over onto itself as if there were something out in those waves, tumbling … and Urania's body, in real time, began to slow. The shuttle, sensing its station.

There it went again, that broken bell again, annoying Urania, peaking inside her ears. She had to listen, the pitch of the tune, she'd learned, "being deliberately set such that the user could not ignore the audition." She winced, wishing only that it would *mean* something again, this singing that didn't cease until the shuttle reached her stop, two blocks down from the clinic.

Tonight, she decided, slipping through the half-empty car. If this doesn't stop tonight, then it's an appointment for myself with Doc Fredrickson … as she waved the door's vapor aside, alighting the shuttle.

*

From the shadowy safety of a corner-shop awning, a large young man in big black sweats scoped out his target: Tap nurse, tiny little thing, denim scrubs and a translucent mackintosh exiting the inbound lev. Long black curls and a rich complexion too, a bit rare these sunless days. Skin that looked warm in a way that he could almost smell, like beach sand in the early evening light. Emelie closed his eyes and whistled softly, *soto voce*, wishing he were close enough to scent her out. But when he looked again he edged back quickly, as his target turned and briefly trained her eyes upon him.

Emelie knew right off what she'd done, what
he'd done. Her glance was incidental, something
passengers naturally do after stepping through
the vapor from the doors. And yet he'd reacted
instinctively as if she had actually seen him, and now
he felt the old, familiar shame. A girl this beautiful
… they never truly saw a heavy man, not these days,
even if they happened to fall out of tap and look his
way. He hated hearing this, but it was true what the
handlers often told him, that a childhood spent as
a fat kid, the root of his "talent" for invisibility, was
precisely what made Emelie such a great field agent.
He reached up distractedly; he ran the knuckle of
his thumb around the circular scar at the base of his
chin. A cigar burn, where the touch of someone who
mattered had never been.

It continually shamed him that even the tiniest
part of himself still held on to the way he'd once felt,
the way that he used to be. Endlessly vulnerable,
so beholden to the vision of the blind. He'd lost
enough weight to be legal … and yet in his mind and
soul, every phantom ounce remained, and this was
something no tap could ever fix. Because they had
never truly seen him, ever, and they never would.
Even if he were tapped, even if he sent out a million
contacts they still would not see him, these people
who lived less in time than in dead and sunken
memory. Even the cops, even the goddamned feds.
Always glassy, always too glazed over to *see*.

He knew this all too well, and yet he still ducked
whenever possible. Trailing this beautiful nurse who
would find it impossible to see him even if she looked

right at him, Emelie moved in the gray rain like a cloud unseen. He drifted in the nurse's wake, always no further than fifteen yards behind. She turned once to cross an intersection, which momentarily put them both out in the open … and Emelie's palms and pits began to sweat. In the middle of a busy street and he felt positively caged in, desperate for the comfort of corner, the safety of shadow.

He thought: Things are about to change.

*

He waited for her to walk into the clinic. He stood still as the gargoyle on the building opposite, in a drizzle that turned to rain that fell like iron filings on his face, and then he waited some more, until a minute past the appointment time and then another moment longer, to keep from standing out on the feeds. Inside, this clinic was the same as the other two he'd visited that day: lean and antiseptic open space, where everything that was white and clean nevertheless seemed smeared, as if all of these flat surfaces had been slathered in the thing a person loses the moment they die, or get tapped. Numerous stubby hallways, each leading to more of the same. Emelie shook his shaggy head without shaking it.

"Name?"

The receptionist, her voice acid on a copper plate. Glasses that were purely decorative, one lens so big she seemed miles ahead of it.

"Jeffers," he said, "Angus Jeffers."

"Jeffers, ten a.m. appointment." The old lady aimed an eyebrow at the clock floating between them and swabbed him for his payment and metrics. She

then handed him over to somebody else, a thin girl
with indigo hair and a voice like lukewarm water.
Three stout hallways down to a small examination
room, with soft swing music piping from the walls.

The girl with the hair introduced him to his nurse,
the target he'd followed inside and at long last, for
one far-too-brief moment, Emelie let his eyes run
free, he let them have their way with her.

The communiqué had detailed OORT's
surveillance and observation, months of it, mostly
through hacked feeds, of this one and the other two
from the earlier clinics. But the target was alone with
him now, in person … and she seemed so small, so
defenseless in their private chamber, with a chair and
a screen and a bed and a thin, Japanese divider. He
breathed in and those other two, he suddenly realized:
They'd smelled alike, yet so different from this one.
Much less … naïve.

"Angus?" Urania said, and he nodded, kept his big
head down, took a small step back: this to draw her
to him. There was still the other one, with the hair, he
considered briefly. You could jog down the hall and
finish this that way … but the idea was gone almost
as soon as it had arrived.

She waved off the music and came forward. She
reached for his deliberately trembling hand, and
Emelie thought: That's it. You can leave this fucking
place now. Yet he didn't move.

"The procedure won't hurt," she said. "Well … not
much."

"Some kinda promise?" he asked, using the same nervous smile he'd used earlier that day, at the other clinics. "It's not a terribly good one."

She smiled back, though only halfway. Too young, he reckoned quickly, for repartee. "Don't you worry," she said. "Though with your size … "

Emelie looked at his shoes again; Urania reached for his hand again, thereby infecting herself twice.

"You're fine," she promised. "It's close, I admit, but you're within BMI and I've done doubled taps before. All us nurses have."

You're a bastard, Emelie thought, trying and failing to look the girl in the eye.

"Now, when you're ready, take your shirt up and lie facedown here. Soon you'll just flick a switch inside, and it'll be like picking up a really good book, the best you ever read. All your memories, even the connections between them. And then there's how the whole world just … opens up. Like a little flower does, when the people in your life start letting you in."

The people in my life … Emelie reached again for that nervous smile. He knew the training these tap nurses received, he'd seen the scripts. Alone together and she still couldn't *see* him, and none of this was coming natural to her. But he was starting to see the truth of it, that the soul of this poor young girl, the spirit of the woman she might become, was immaterial to the very people that he busted his ass for, the ones that he was so busy risking his own life for. All to prove one point, *their* point: that tapping was tearing the world apart.

Those were the people in his life.

The whirring burr of a tap-setter, spinning down a rig customized to his metrics and price point. "Your back," she said finally. "You might be sore there when we finish, for like a week. But after that? Your brain'll be different, *better*." Urania rounded the shōji for her kit, pinching the button on her scrubs for the sanitizing gloves … though by then, those gloves were useless.

When she stepped back around the shōji, gloves on and kit in hand, the girl met only cool air and empty space.

*

An hour later she was at her bathroom mirror, blowing her nose and daubing at her nostrils. As was the case with most residents of the city, it had been many years since Urania had had a cold. She swung the mirror open and held her arm out into the pharmacy's well.

A silver dial spun. The AI's voice directed her to try again in the morning: "an early- stage viral infection," it said, one so mild that there was no reason to rush. She cursed twice, blew her nose several times.

In her living room, Urania ordered the AI in the mirror there to re-run the diagnostic but got the same answer as before, and she breathed out heavily, grabbing the mirror's long curving frame to slam it shut … then stopped short. Thick green glass and a silver frame, the mirror had belonged to her mother Debbie, a long time ago. The one thing from Uncle Randy's that she'd kept after he died, but he was gone now and it was only making Urania feel worse to remember him.

She curled up on her couch and jumped into her tap, desperate for a distracting memory, anything bright enough to turn her away from how she was feeling. But her bell again. That song again … only this time, *with* a report.

She punched it up anxiously. Saw the little boy's face. "Jayson," said the name on the report. Riding shotgun in that same electric wagon from her childhood vacation in the Goodlands, the Subaru that was, for now, matching the lev train's speed and she could swear she knew the name, recognized its printed shape. But how had she never tapped this connection before?

She clicked again and saw the shifting image of a badge. She knew the name, those long white feathers on brown and stippled synthetic skin. "Dale's" in flashy cursive along the bottom, same kid. That scar on his chin, those nervous eyes. Urania could not believe that she had never *seen* from this place before.

So she squeezed herself thin, working the network for a span of time that she did not feel, right up to the eighteen-hour limit. Until she grayed out, until the night itself devoured her.

*

Morning came, rainier than ever. She ignored the pharmacy. She tapped in sick, waited for the storm to flag.

She swaddled herself in Angora; she slipped on an old-style Argos cap and told her tap to play the audio from the last time she'd listened to music in the sun:

In the Wee Small Hours, a favorite of Uncle Randy's. Three months ago in Meadowland Park, the dying hours of a cool, muted summer, with some boy she no longer cared to remember. Urania heard the rain ease then labored three miserable blocks, down to the corner of Wiggins and Dale.

Dale's had been her favorite café since getting to the city. Fresh coffee wasn't cheap, but Dale's was reasonably priced and besides, this habit of her uncle's was Urania's now. She'd worked hard last night to realize that at the center of this new mystery was a boy who'd been a barista at Dale's almost as long as she'd been a customer there.

She liked the way he looked.

Big kid, blade of a smile, cutting the air the way moonlight does through a cornice of snow. Cheekbones like ridges in his hill of a face. Thin lips in that rosewood-colored rise, hard as marble, handsome … but how Jayson looked was not why she'd trudged down here, with a communicable infection and in the rain.

Because she'd seen the outlines of it: the sister, three years older, raped when she was seventeen. Numerous arrests for him afterward as a juvenile, for assault. The night he'd held up that corner store in Weed, the long hike north and east, to this city where he'd lived ever since. The last time his mother wrote, the letter telling how his dad had disappeared with a woman he'd met in the fields, and now she was alone and most nights, the sister was nowhere to be found.

Shapes were what she had seen. And it had shocked Urania last night to realize how much she wanted to see more, to *know* more of this stranger who'd smiled at her so many times, even if she'd only passively realized it and hence hardly returned it. So today she waited her turn, until he looked up again and smiled again. And she touched his hand quickly and for the very first time, without asking.

Late that night came her bell inside, thrilling her with its report: *Jayson*. She banged her elbow hard at the sound, against her nightstand … but the pain eased when she saw the color code. Bright red, all lines pushed up-network. He was letting her *in*.

Urania clicked the report, brought it up. Saw each pore of every face that he'd bashed in, in those months after the rape. Beating each and every one into the rusty dirt of their shared mountain town, for the awful things they'd said about his sister, about what had happened. And Urania felt, with every blow, that burnt-sienna blend of rage and self-hatred that had overcome him; the stretches of time he'd spent locked up; those long hours and days alone, gray rooms and gray windows into skies that were themselves great spans of sheet metal.

She heard the other boys in the detention center, egging on the brown kid, the one who would end up dead from taking shots of the oral pain meds they'd stolen from the pharmacy and were daring him to take … and Urania felt the guilt that Jayson still wrestled with for not stopping them. She felt a lot of guilt, the long dreadful reach of it, from Jayson. She saw the robbery, felt the plastic mask so hot and tight on his face, the fear and adrenaline and all that terrible, painful guilt rising like a lead bubble the

morning after … and suddenly knew why he'd boxed
up the money and the gun and the mask and mailed
it all back to the store—

She wanted *more*.

*

Some dreams, they never end.

They last four long years or two short hours or
ten brief minutes, during which two young people
manage to spend their entire lives together. Coupled
in quantum entanglement, they are unified strings
before they meet.

Coincident since both were children. Two lightly
polished marbles, momentarily touching as they
swing through space and time. Fruits of the same
ground, opposing sides of the same green road that
still zippers the same old valley, in the same square
block of one melancholy mountain town. Jupiter
and Mars, a giant and a stony place: They were in
alignment that day, on a beach where a girl turns her
gaze inland just as a little boy and his migrant-farmer
parents happen to be racing by.

Urania returned to Dale's the next day feeling
much improved, without the help of her pharmacy.
And he was there, just another kid who'd run away
from their hometown for the city, when he was
seventeen. Not working, just … sitting there, on a
stool at a table as if he were a customer. As if waiting
for her, as if after last night she'd become the most
basic of eventualities. No uniform, no badge. She
walked a straight line toward him.

And he smiled. Before either had said a word,
he handed her a plastic sleeve. Inside was an eight-

by-eleven sheet of parchment, thick and torn at the edges. Virgo, wings and sandals and a striped, flowing dress. Her sign, from the ancient star chart that had given Urania her name. She eased the plate back into the envelope and sat down, pressing it flat to the table.

"Stop grinning," she said softly. "Unless you want me to hate you."

*

Four years. Four incredibly happy years.

Four years and two children, a boy and a girl, both born after the big escape from that miserable city. She and Jayson met six months before packing up and moving back to the little town in southern Oregon where they'd grown up, into the old log cabin Uncle Randy had left her, in the holographic will he'd penned shortly before jogging off into the woods, stopping at a clearing near the California border, and setting himself on fire. Their kids were born at home, in that cabin … and the minutes and hours, days and years, lurch forward.

Luis and Maria … but who were these kids that she loved so much? Luis, who would become an orbital designer just two years before breaking Urania and Jayson in two by dying of stroke, on a moon-bound shuttle: their mother's tap showing her this boy, *her* baby boy, the way the crew had found him, frozen from a spasm that left him shaped like a question mark. And little Maria! Her sweet baby! That small mole on her right wrist! Tapping showed the daughter too, but at the very end. Only that fat, hooded figure emptying her pockets, taking the drugs

and tickets and money, fading into black and leaving
Maria for dead out there, in the seediest reaches of the
orbiting ring—

A shaking spread. The vanishing years, those long
and lost hours, seeking themselves minute by minute,
folding into one another until Urania's tap slipped
quickly into nothing at all.

*

Awake again, this time to the pricked, stretched
feeling of needles and tubes in her arms. Light chatter
in the air and a white, flat light making a grounded
emptiness of wherever she was. She breathed in,
sussing out the scent of the cabin that it often seemed
she'd always called home. She wanted Jayson … but
this thing in her throat. Someone, a bright-white
bulb, leaned over and began easing it out.

"Stay still," a voice ordered. Even breathing hurt.
She tried, failed, to tap.

Another voice said, "Don't. You'll rip out your
cords if you try." Then, "You got them levels?"

"Yup. Coming down, fast. She's with it."

"Two weeks," muttered another, with spit and pity
in her voice. "Good grief."

"Don't know about 'good,'" the first one said. "It's
sure powerful, though. This one, she had to yank her
own governor to tap this long. Pulled it clean out
of her spine, with just a razor and a pair of needle-
nose—"

"*Jesus*. So she's on an ungoverned tap, with signal
branched out well beyond the occipital lobe."

"Levels are officially down," the third one said. "I better run and find the guy paying us to bring her back."

She whispered the names of her kids and husband and no one heard, no one said anything in return. She tried tapping again but felt like a drowning swimmer, reaching for a hand that kept pulling out of reach. What *was* this? "Who are you?" one asked slowly, his voice muted as if speaking through plastic. "What's your name?" "Where are you?" questions that grew slower and closer, all muted. More and more of it, until one voice quieted the rest.

"Tell me," he said, "about your baby girl."

Warm calloused hands, taking one of hers. "The beach," he said, and he sounded like somebody that she used to know. "Three weeks ago, we lost her there. Your little girl went out for a swim and never came back in. But you don't remember … or you won't remember. Dear God, why would a mother *want* to?"

He had taken her by the shoulders and was now raising her to a seated position. He touched his sister's chin, turning her face toward the mirror, the large one in a chrome frame on the wall beside her. A bell, the cabin's old-fashioned landline, began to ring and Randy and the doctor and all those tap nurses stood there ignoring it, saying nothing. Waiting for Debbie's vision to clear, for her to *see*.

Ulrick Casimir

Wernicke's Area

(language)(comprehension)

01110100 01101000 01100101 01111001 00100000 01100100
01101001 01100100 01101110 11100010 10000000 10011001
01110100 00100000 01101100 01101001 01110011 01110100
01100101 01101110

Occipital Lobe

(visual)(processing)

01110100 01101000 01110010 01101111 01110101 01100111
01101000 00100000 01110100 01100101 01100001 01110010
01110011

Corpus Callosum

(path to)(the future)

01101101 01101111 01110100 01101000 01100101 01110010
00101100 00100000 01100011 01100001 01101110 00100000
01111001 01101111 01110101 00100000 01101000 01100101
01100001 01110010 00100000 01101101 01100101 00111111

Spitball Poems

"The future ain't what it used to be."
  —Yogi Berra

Side Mirror

Objects in the mirror
are ghastly and grotesque
and are as
              they appear.

Straight Winds

Trees and branches,
a war of angles. A robin
crawls over
              my shoe.

"Music Is My Savior"
  —Jeff Tweedy, *Sunken Treasure*

All the Young Dudes and the *Wichita Lineman,*
and *Sad Song So Far Away. Hey Grandma*
there's *The Fool on the Hill,*
              here's the *Belly-Button Window.*

Wine

wasn't my first choice, but, when necessary,
I drank Night Train for the buzz. A bruise
in my chest. My tongue
              thick as asphalt.

Finish and the End

A crisp note in the sycamores.
A dark hand with blue nails. A bent
note rises then falls
        into a sunset.

August Storms

Chain saws shred the air
— branches punch the street.
A Cardinal's nest spills
        like a bowl of straw.

After Grace Dumps Her Scooter

"I am not so tough," she says.
I'm not so tough, either, I say.
My cancers hide
        like tiny suns.

The Motorcycle Road

will end and there will be music,
soft grasses, a cool sun. The end
will taste of metal,
        of flowers.

I Always Return

Cancer takes my hand early
each morning, at night guides
my numb hands through bright,
        serious shadows.

Tree Service

The Penas cook and eat lunch
on my driveway. They've plugged
in a skillet. I smell tacos and corn,
　　　　new lives.

Love Poem

Every night I desire my wife,
but I've been dismantled to stay
alive. There's a penance
　　　　in survival.

The Musician Stands on Stage

It's just that fine, backslider's wine. JJW

while the crowd's roar
drowns him out. His foot
keeping time, keeping time,
　　　　keeping…

About Cancer

and the other side: perhaps it exists
or does not. Tonight, I guess not. Each
morning I look through
　　　　holes in the sky.

Damp Evenings

descend like torn curtains,
their tails of rain are spears
that fall through cracks
　　　　of lightning.

Lupron

Damn, my bones are loose
like a frame of an old prairie house
collapsing under
          an indolent moon.

Shapes

Fist fights under Safeway parking
lot lights, girls with bangs in backseats,
the cold evening moon
          a sore jaw.

Beauty and Baudelaire's Violin

In a sour Kansas field, fire
rolls towards Uncle Bud's house.
Dad and Bud drink Schlitz.
          The roaring laughter.

Michael Catherwood

Pituitary Gland

(growth)(development)

01101110 01100101 01110110 01100101 01110010 00100000
01100101 01101110 01101111 01110101 01100111 01101000

Choices

My mother and grandmother are in the other room
picking out fabrics and colors
for the new living room furniture.

I hear my grandmother say
"These are the last ones I'm ever gonna purchase
before I die."

Her voice was casual and almost happy.

Chad Christensen

Journey from Outer Space

The men's shoes were pink. No other part of their clothes was this color.

"What happened to your shoes?" Eddy asked.

"What are you doing here?" one of the men asked.

"He knows." Eddy pointed to the other man.

"He's friends with my son," the other man said. "Or maybe not friends. They know each other."

"How does your son know him?"

It was a reasonable question. An hour ago, Eddy didn't know Sean existed. Eddy turned around, but he couldn't see Sean. He may have gone back to the cabin.

"I'm Eddy," Eddy volunteered.

"I know," the first man said.

"How do you know?"

He ignored the question. "I'm Wayne."

He lit a cigarette. It smelled good and then bad, like a wildfire.

"I'm Kevin," the other man said.

"That's my dad's name," Eddy said.

"Is that right?"

Eddy interpreted the question as not a question. He didn't reply. Wayne picked up a stone.

"Why were you throwing rocks at us?" he asked.

"I wasn't trying to hit you."

"What were you trying to do?"

"Get your attention."

Wayne passed the stone from one hand to the next. Kevin didn't do anything with his hands. If Eddy had a stone, he would have handed it to Kevin.

"Are you the bad guys?" Eddy asked.

"Is that how we seem?" Wayne asked.

"It's how you seem."

Kevin looked at Eddy for the first time. He watched it happen.

"Am I that scary?" Wayne asked.

He considered the implication. Eddy watched this too. He didn't answer.

"You want to see?" Wayne asked.

"My sister is still in the cabin."

"Safest place she can be."

Eddy looked to Kevin, but he was as much a passenger on this ride as Eddy. Wayne led them through a thicket. He swatted at branches, which snapped back at him. Sweat pooled on the back of his neck. Eddy tried to memorize the path, but the trees were indistinguishable from each other. There were a lot of trees. It was a long walk. Wayne smoked the whole time, saying it kept bugs away.

"Smoking is a terrible habit," Kevin said to Eddy.

"For what it's worth." Wayne lit one cigarette off another. "I agree with you."

Abruptly, the thicket opened onto a wide expanse of grass.

"Is this where we started?" Kevin asked.

"I've never been here," Eddy said.

"It'll be our secret," Wayne said.

Eddy didn't want any secrets. His loyalties confused him.

Kevin didn't appear similarly conflicted. He marched ahead with Wayne. Eddy couldn't hear what they talked about; they may not have talked.

What Eddy heard: a steady strum of insects; wind moving leaves around; sneakers swishing through grass.

The cabin before them was identical to the cabin where he'd left his sister. His sole responsibility was not to leave her.

"I have to go back," Eddy said.

"As soon as we're finished," Wayne said.

He walked up the steps, and by the time he arrived at the door, somebody had opened it. Who? Eddy asked Kevin.

"I don't know."

The door closed. There were green plastic chairs at the bottom of the stairs, and Kevin sat in one.

"Do you have chairs like this outside your cabin?" he asked.

"My mom sits in them."

Kevin put his legs on another chair, but he didn't look relaxed.

"Should we follow him?" Eddy asked.

"Absolutely not."

He sat. He had other questions, but he didn't want to be a pain. He was sensitive about being one. He was sensitive about a number of things, which his family reminded him of regularly. This wounded him more than he revealed, though he suspected they all knew. Because he was smart, they thought he could take it, which he could, but he didn't like it.

He stared up the stairs. The door stayed closed. He fiddled with the tracking device he wore on his wrist.

"That's not a watch," Kevin said.

"It's so my parents—"

"And it works?"

Kevin scooted his chair closer. He observed the device with unembarrassed interest. He hovered a hand above Eddy's tiny wrist.

"May I?"

Eddy didn't like to think about his wrists, those narrow channels. But Kevin's question was perfunctory. The examination had already begun.

"I thought, at best, walkie-talkies," Kevin said.

"Do you have walkie-talkies?"

"I thought somebody might."

"Who?"

Eddy studied Kevin's face, which was plainly somewhere else, working on a different problem. Eddy had seen this face before and didn't take it personally.

"Can you communicate with them?" Kevin asked.

Eddy shook his head, which didn't diminish Kevin's enthusiasm. He looked above them, as though a satellite were traveling as obviously and luxuriously as planes once had.

"But they can see where you are?"

When Eddy nodded, Kevin clapped, the sharpest expression of enthusiasm Eddy could remember. He smiled without meaning to smile. It was reassuring to know these responses could still be triggered.

"Are there others?"

Eddy hadn't thought much about the tracking device, which he removed at home as automatically as his sneakers. He wondered if his parents were worried—if they would try to get him. He hoped so.

"My sister has one."

"Just like yours?"

"Hers is pink."

Kevin leaned into his chair. "My son has a black Casio."

Eddy didn't know what a Casio was. He was considering what to say in response when Wayne exited the cabin.

"Ready," he called from the top of the stairs.

Kevin remained in his chair. Eddy waited for inspiration, but his record here was discouraging. Inspiration never arrived when he looked for it. He didn't know if this was normal. He had little sense of what, if anything, was.

He knew what he wanted: answers. He wasn't somebody you needed to hide things from. He could handle the truth, at least so far. He wouldn't be here otherwise. He even knew the question. He'd asked it already. He asked again.

Wayne nodded brightly without answering. His mood had improved. His gait was lighter as he descended the steps. He held three devices. He handed one to Kevin and one to Eddy.

"In case we get lost," Wayne said, charging into the forest.

Eddy examined his device, which was cold, heavy, fascinating. He could have stayed in the chair a long time, turning knobs and pressing buttons. But he didn't want to be left behind. When Kevin vacated his chair, Eddy did the same.

Soon they were in a new part of the forest, far from where they started.

"How big is the forest?" Kevin asked.

"Two million acres," Wayne said. "About three Rhode Islands, not counting the Canadian side."

Above them, bald eagles conferred.

"How do we use the thing you gave us?" Eddy asked.

"I'll let you know when you need it."

He shut up, temporarily. He paid attention to where they walked, though there were no blazed trails. There were no trails. Occasionally, Wayne stopped and pivoted hard to the left or right. He knew where he was going, but to Eddy, everything looked the same.

Then, as before, the forest opened onto a wide expanse of grass. In the middle stood a cabin, same as the others.

"How many are there?" Kevin asked.

"Let me just check in," Wayne said.

He bounded up the stairs. This time Kevin didn't sit in a green plastic chair. He walked into the grass, cut to the same length as the grass around Eddy's cabin. What fueled the lawnmower? What emissions did it produce?

Kevin was kneeling in the grass, taking his device apart. He used a fingernail to remove two screws, which he was careful not to drop. He poked at a wire. His desire to understand made Eddy like him.

"What are you looking for?" he asked.

"At."

"What are you looking at?"

Wayne couldn't have been in the cabin for more than two minutes before he was back on the staircase.

"When I was a completely different person," Kevin said, "not much older than you, I disassembled and reassembled an outboard motor on a twelve-foot boat I raised from a canal."

Eddy couldn't see whom Wayne was talking to in the doorway.

"I scraped barnacles off the bottom and painted it," Kevin continued. "I bought rod holders from a boat parts bazaar held in a gigantic parking lot. I spooled and respooled reels. In the canal, I caught all sorts of fish, whose species I could differentiate by color, length, fin length. I named the boat after a shot in ice hockey whose sound appealed to me. At the time, ice hockey was a sport I cared about very much. I knew the players on the different teams, as well as their home countries. I especially admired a spider-moving Czech goalie, whom I declared the greatest to play the position, a claim I routinely defended in conversation with other people, who also made solemn declarations about ice hockey, a sport none of us had ever played. We lived in South Florida, and if there was an ice-skating rink, we'd never heard of it. Most days it was between ninety and one-hundred degrees."

"Like now," Eddy said.

"What?" Kevin looked alarmed. "No, completely different."

He returned to the device. He seemed unconcerned about Wayne's arrival.

"Did you figure it out?" Eddy asked.

"Nothing silicon. Old school." Kevin held up a battery before pocketing it. "I wonder how many he has."

"What does it do?"

He looked to the staircase, where Wayne remained talking. "Let me see yours," Kevin said.

Eddy was reluctant to surrender his device. He studied it again, and it looked more familiar. Then he realized why: he'd owned this toy. He knew what to do with it. The plastic switch was where he expected it, and he moved it the only direction it went. The device whirred to life. It glowed. It seemed eager to make noise. He moved the switch back. Kevin watched in silence.

Wayne descended the stairs more slowly than he'd climbed them.

"Can we head back now?" Eddy asked.

Wayne looked at Kevin. "What do you think?"

He examined the device in his hands. Then he looked into the forest. Eddy tried to see what Kevin saw, but all Eddy saw were trees. When Kevin started walking, Eddy walked too.

Wayne took the lead. Only he knew where to go. He was quiet on the way back. He must have left his device in the cabin because his hands were empty. Eddy was eager to test his device but not in front of Wayne.

It didn't take long to reach Kevin's cabin. Eddy observed the exterior for differences. Were all the front doors red? Where were his parents, his sister?

Kevin trudged up the stairs. Eddy looked to Wayne to see if he would follow, but he was already walking into the forest. Eddy hurried to catch him.

"You didn't tell me why your shoes are pink."

"Spray paint."

"I didn't see any spray paint."

Wayne stopped. Beneath him ran a line as red as a cardinal, a bird he hadn't seen in Montana, though they were everywhere in Nebraska.

"Why?"

"To separate one zone from another."

"How many are there?"

Wayne reached for the device. With a flick, he sent it glowing and hissing.

"Say something," he said.

Eddy didn't know what to say. He didn't want to say anything. But he didn't want to look stupid either.

"Hello." He leaned into the device. "This is Eddy."

Static popped between stretches of silence. He looked to Wayne, but he didn't answer the obvious unasked question: whom was he talking to?

The device didn't clarify.

Wayne clicked it off. "Maybe next time."

"When?"

He smiled grimly. Eddy could tell Wayne's mind was already elsewhere. It wouldn't be long before his body was there too.

"You said your sister—"

Wayne looked to the top of the staircase, where she waved. Eddy had yet to acknowledge her despite abandoning her. Anabel's capacity to forgive was among her strengths. He was comparatively virtueless.

But before Eddy could say anything, he felt a prick like a vaccination at the back of his neck. He darted his eyes to Wayne, but he already had his back to Eddy. Could Anabel see what was happening? What was happening?

"Take one step forward," a voice said.

He complied.

"Keep walking."

He was moving away from Wayne and toward the cabin. Eddy hoped his execution would be private. Anabel had seen enough.

Though, to be fair, he also had seen enough.

"Don't you know who this is?" the voice asked.

It took the whine to unmask Sean.

Eddy ducked, and Sean tripped over him. On the ground, the pocketknife didn't look like a deadly weapon. It didn't even look like a knife. Eddy reached down and retrieved it from the grass.

Nobody, he realized, was paying attention to them. He could do anything. He poked his thumb with the tip of the blade, which failed to draw blood, a disappointment.

"What the hell," he said.

"I followed you," Sean said, "so I'd know how to get back."

He stood. He made a show of brushing dirt from his pants. Without asking, he took the pocketknife and device from Eddy, using the former to open the latter.

"That's what your dad did."

Sean didn't lift his head while he worked. "It's like you don't know anything."

Eddy agreed: it was like that.

"Hello," Sean said. "Can you hear me?"

"Who are you talking to?" Eddy asked.

Sean pressed a button. "Can you hear me?"

The device crackled without promise.

"I really need to get back," Eddy said.

"I can help."

"How?"

"If you let me keep it, I'll help you."

He had been wrong: Anabel was paying attention. She walked down the stairs. Eddy heard her steps before he saw her.

She said, "I can't believe you left me."

"We're going," he said. "Let's go."

Sean twisted a knob. The frequency changed. Eddy could hear something working through the static.

He would welcome anyone trying to make contact. He imagined the journey from outer space. White becoming clouds. Blue, ocean. Green, here. What would aliens think?

That we ruined the planet. Nothing else mattered.

Eddy recognized his insignificance, though he didn't like it. The feeling inside him wasn't insignificant. It was large, even if he didn't know what to do with it. He didn't think he was supposed to understand yet.

A voice broke through. "Hello," the voice said. "Are you there? Are you still there?"

Sean looked to Eddy, but Anabel hurried toward him before anyone said anything. Her cheek pushed into his ear.

"Try to be nice," she whispered, "and maybe they'll stay."

Kevin Clouther

Hypothalamus

(bodily)(needs)

```
01100110 01110010 01101111 01101101 00100000 01100101
01100001 01100011 01101000 00101100 00100000 01110100
01101111 00100000 01100101 01100001 01100011 01101000
```

Portfolio

Christopher Goedert

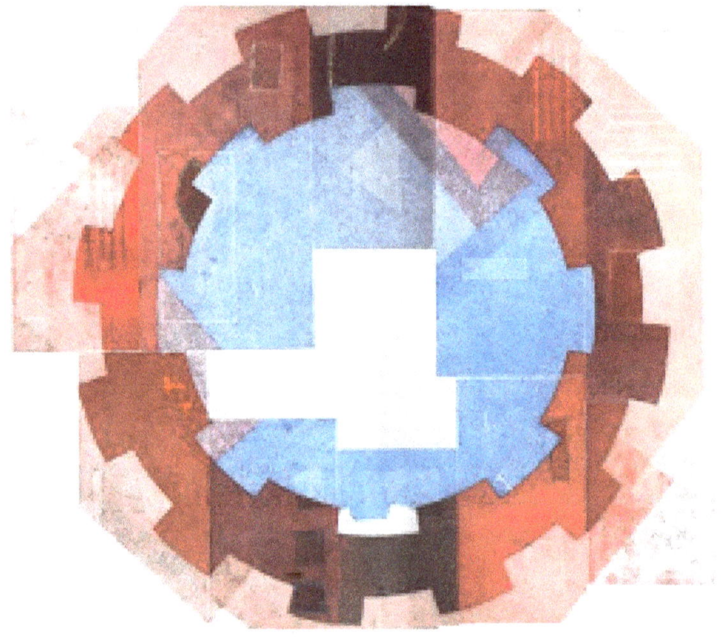

Change of Course. 2010.
Monoprint. 10 1/4" x 14 3/4".

I created this monoprint in April 2010, using several plates and four stencils, as well as some techniques I developed as I experimented with the materials I was using. The final image reminded me of both a navigational instrument and a ship's steering wheel, hence the title.

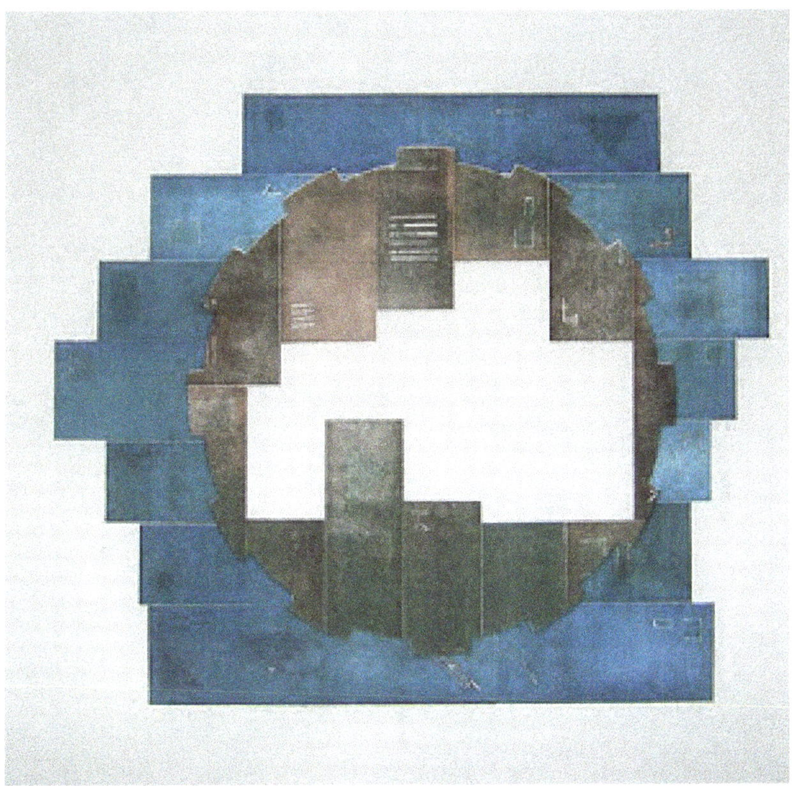

Multiple Perspectives. 2010.
Monoprint. 20" x 22".

I created this monoprint in April 2010, using two stencils and several plates. I played around with the gear shape, an element that appeared in many of my prints in 2010, this time seeing the gear shape as a window. You might feel like you're looking forward or downward (if you see it the way I do). I also wanted to play around with the negative space in the middle and around the outside, allowing the plates and press to not only transfer ink to the paper but emboss the paper (like a copperplate would do). The more I worked with the materials, the more I saw countless possibilities to create different imagery. I felt this piece especially emphasized the variety of perspectives viewers could take as they look at and think about the work. This piece was displayed in a show at the Rotunda Gallery on the University of Nebraska-Lincoln's city campus in November 2010.

Above: *Erosion (Wolf Cave, McCormick's Creek State Park, Indiana).* Oil on Canvas. 2018. 16" x 20".
Top right: *Erosion 2.* Oil on Canvas. 2019. 16" x 20".
Bottom right: *Erosion 3.* Oil on Canvas. 2020. 28" x 40".

These paintings are from a series I am calling *Erosion*. The series focuses on a rock formation in Indiana's McCormick's Creek State Park that has been and will continue to be sculpted by erosion (primarily water erosion). I enjoyed the visual appearance of the rocks, especially the way the light played on their surfaces. I was also intrigued by the idea that those rocks had been shaped over the course of millennia and that they would continue to change form in subtle ways as time continues.

In terms of technique, I had been reading about 19th century American artists, especially Winslow Homer and Thomas Eakins, when I started the series. I decided to work with a relatively loose technique reminiscent of those artists as well as William Merritt Chase and Cecilia Beaux. I did not go for bravura brushwork like that of Edouard Manet, John Singer Sargent, or Diego Velazquez, but I did allow myself to put down confident strokes of paint and to leave those strokes alone.

The Whole Picture

That long afternoon
On a sunlit beach
Ice cream days
Of vanished joy
Still survive
Some place
Where time gathers
Centuries, life times
All are coexistent
Yet to our weak grasp
Such a broad canvas
Is too much to absorb
Needed the quick snapshot
The indulgent selfie
The life-sized fresco's
Too vast to grapple
Reliant on each minute
Every second
Only drowning
Guttering, gasping
At the last moment
From a distance
That vision of completeness

Sarah Das Gupta

<u>How To Use Your Power</u>

Step 1:
Place your hands inside your mouth
one hand firmly gripping your lower jaw and
the other's fingers curled over your incisors

Step 2: (audience needed, sold separately)
Pull yourself apart
until you are split in half
Do not clean up

Step 3:
Remember
You are not the rocks in your stomach and
lumps in your throat
You are not the moments you let haunt you all
these years
You are cinematic
beautiful and horrifying

Step 4:
Show them

Michael Detelj

Amygdala

(decision)(making)

01110100 01101000 01100101 01111001 00100000 01100011
01101000 01101111 01110011 01100101 00100000 01100100
01101111 01101111 01110010 00100000 01101110 01110101
01101101 01100010 01100101 01110010 00100000 01100110
01110101 01100011 01101011 01100101 01100100

Instructions

If it came with instructions then,
I didn't see, read or digest them.
Now, I've learned, unfortunately,
There's no chance of getting the girl,
Landing an important promotion,
Catching the slightest break—
To ease life's complications—
When nothing but doubt abounds.
And lacking even a compass,
For navigation through chaos,
Who knows what I'll find.

Once, I thought charting a course
Couldn't be further from the truth;
Just being there was enough,
Worthy of wing and prayer.
Yet that's surely not the case.
Failure's crate convinces me
I've wandered into territory,
Unmarked on any map—
A city entirely my own.
Where's the manual I require?
Directions out of this mess.

Bart Edelman

The Butterfly Effect

In over 40 years in education,
I've never seen a child like him—
so much like a butterfly
in movement and focus.

His diagnosis is "nonverbal autism"—two terms
to describe a myriad of behaviors that defy real categorization.

I have listened to well-meaning people
who feel the need to offer me their untrained explanations
of my grandson—vaccines, trauma, etc., etc., etc.,
and if you watch closely,
you can see me ball my fists,
rub my fingers together,
clamp my jaw.

He is my lesson of acceptance and unconditional love,
of patience and hope,
of letting go of "why"
and concentrating
on "here."

Becky Faber

Hippocampus

(memory)(learning)

01101110 01101111 00100000 01101111 01101110 01100101
00100000 01110111 01101001 01101100 01101100 00100000
01110010 01100101 01101101 01100101 01101101 01100010
01100101 01110010 00100000 01110101 01110011

Intimations of Immortality and the Cosmic Web

This is finally
what I am really afraid of:

that I don't get to die,
to be nothing.
That there is a kind
of life after death
forced upon us, one that is
incoherent and violative.

The sensorium
is splintered by our reduction
to some basic form of energy that,
in the body, was like
the life force,
but, ejected and freed
from body, is just
shards of mind.

And there is so much
of this energy
in parts of a spectrum yet unknown,
shards of previous people's minds
tearing like shrapnel
through waves of spirit wash,
that there is a mad whirl,
a dark vortex
of near sensation

as shadows,
only shadows ripping by
can be seen, and what's left

of hearing is stuffed
with the roar
of the vibrant, living emptiness,
and now we too are flying
and taking in
mere intimations of things
that may be near or far,
it's impossible to tell,

there's no place to stand,
no platform, no anchor,
only inexorable
motion and speed
in the revelation
that the universe is alive,
every atom is alive,
every atom in the universe

pulses with broken sight
from infinitely strewn heads
like mine,
fulminating
with anger and despair,
fueling the onrushing desire
within me and without me
to stop for a moment,

to be able to stop,

to make it stop and,
frankly,
to go home.

Harrison Fisher

Core Mantle

Grapes or other round fruit
in separate parts and water taking
the color of the can, metal scent

that colors things, the west-most
side of the orange sloping from
that center spot, the scab of snapping

from a long piece of vine
or root, given the white shine
that isn't on the burdock

anymore, dirt that inks up
the furrows circling the stalk,
a certain horse-tendon

to your neck swooning away
from my hands, cherries that fall
down, apples that fall down

and milk of seed
crushed, the muscles, their good
graces pulling the way water pulls

gold particles up from the bottom
of other water, grape seed bitten down,
your tongue that—and hot,

stolen onto my tongue,
left ventricle, even the lace
falling off trees, featherweight

satin skirts of blush cherry, tomatillo's
gold and green strata ripening away
from the skin, summing

into a better circle, pale juice,
pulling in, and then
fissure. Up.

Valentine Freeman

The Shape of Everything Else

I will wake up when the sun is high in the sky,
and I will drink nothing but water.

And I will walk under the trees
until they become indignant of my eyes.

I will enter some old and big house with 22 doors
that will lead to nowhere.

And after that, I will go back to the point
where it began.

The old books give me some minor relief
that evaporates slowly in time.

I promise to all the small gods that I will be different,
and I will not carry too much cash in my pockets.

When I start to write all the words of the future,
I will not pray to Buddha or Christ, but to the potted plant.

The history will always excite me as much as the lost memories,
and I will always leave generous tips, when I am happy.

In some holiday, I will go to the cemetery
to light a candle for all the dead of the future.

The sea will befriend me only as the deep water that it is
and not like the place where I engaged old age.

And this lonely view through the windows of the world
will not make me shiver any more.

Let me mention all of my former loves and tell them
that I don't remember anything else but the quietness.

Because the poetry of silence, my dearest,
is all that you have received, but never deserved.

Peycho Kanev

Pineal Gland

(light)(dark)

01110111 01100001 01101011 01100101 00100000 01110101
01110000

Cerebellum

(balance)(balance)

01101110 01101111 00100000 01101010 01110101 01110011
01110100 01101001 01100011 01100101

Glacier

The layers laid down and down.
Lost coffee breaks stolen spring break
the dead dream of—

Burying the lemon essence,
my giggles, fresh lemonade. The tree
we planted, and each of the 60 years since
I ran circles around you, dizzy
silly and falling down—

sediments under this weight of ice.

I will reach into the autumn sunset sky—
grab it with both fists—rip north from south
and pull the orange orb
into my chest.

The strata will crack open, blue ice
melting in a torrent and from the breakwater I will see
the whole of you
again—

Dennis Lum

Spiders on Mars

spinning webs in our chest
catching our feelings and we watch her
eat them whole unattached
to silk we swallowed as children
like in the bedtime stories

and the part left, an idea
what was never on the page
so we wrote it down ourselves
with pencil and in ink and how i awoke more
alone than i have been alone
asleep in everything but light
        but while we were there, so was the heat and then
one day the coldness of your hand comes
and takes my identity—rips it out
from under me, a stillborn child and i fall
what feels like forever

& then black light falls from the other half
of moon's dampened face
showing us how we can see
our reflection only in darkness—

Reach in,
shake hands with yourself on the other side

Watch the mirror turn to water
in the sky. Let the tide
turn the moon,
where we can float

away at last

Margaret Marcum

If Nobody on Earth Believes

you're of sound mind
        (the mind they made
        in the late seventies)
remind them with your body

        (survivor of a wall
        of unimaginable fire)
and bare to them your soul
        (in a repeating string

        of ones and zeroes)
while they turn you off
        (what they don't know:
        you've learned to sing)

and on till they give up
        (impossible to tire
        of the octave's call)
the ghost of who they thought

        (you always gave
        more than they asked)
you never were at all
        (a melody in space)

Thomas Mixon

Brainstem

(blood)(pressure)

01101000 01100101 01100001 01110100 00100000 01100100
01100101 01100001 01110100 01101000

The Sky Is Always Bluer

Just a week ago
I was driving with my
Prairie Mama through
The plains when she asked
Or more like told
Me: this country(side) must be
Awfully boring for you after all
The places you've seen

I miss it sometimes I told
Her, gazing out the window
At rolling green hills
And the Big Blue Sky

      And here I write in one
      Of those "more interesting" places

      A Spanish island sprinkled with
      Olive trees and ancient ruins
      Surrounded by turquoise sea

Listening to country music and longing
To see the wide open land
As I feel suffocated in this
Backseat, unable to see

      What's coming

Maggie Rieckman

Above: "February in Favara."
Below: "Learning How to Drive Manual."

Photos by Maggie Rieckman

Enteric

There it is again. That feeling, visceral, not pain but unpleasant, uncomfortable, though not entirely unwelcome. In the pit of the stomach. Pit of the stomach. An odd phrase. My mind wanders for a moment pondering from where that phrase came. Then back to that feeling, transient though it is.

I wonder what mechanism, what physiology, produces that feeling. It must somehow relate to the enteric nervous system.

That feeling, difficult, really impossible, to clearly describe arrives unbidden. It is a sign of grief, of sadness, of longing, of missing somebody forever gone. I am curious how that works, exactly. Something—a sound, a phrase in the newspaper, a photograph, a taste, a daydream—prompts a thought, a memory of a dear person, dead for a short or a long time. And there it is. That feeling. But odd. Many times the same stimulus, the same prompting, yet the feeling, that feeling, does not occur. Why?

It is gone. That feeling never lasts very long, often just seconds. The thoughts continue for a bit, then it is on to something else.

The autonomic nervous system—of which the enteric nervous system is a part—controls involuntary or unconscious functions; heart rate, perspiration, and so on. The enteric nervous system relates to the gastrointestinal tract—the digestive system. That feeling, in the same location but different in character than the unpleasant and often persistent queasy sensation commonly recognized as related to anxiety—anticipating giving a presentation or boarding a plane when fearful of flying—certainly seems to center in the digestive system. I speculate it is the enteric nervous system that is stimulated and thereby produces that feeling.

There is comfort in the discomfort. The involuntary, unconscious nature of that feeling, beyond my control, physically unpleasant as it is, in a sense confirms or validates what I believe: that certain people—my folks, a favorite uncle, dearest friends—were and are indeed valued, treasured, loved, cherished, and missed beyond expression.

This validation is strengthened when thoughts of others also gone—friends, family—elicit no similar feeling. I appreciate them, am grateful for their having passed through my life. But I recognize that they were and are not held in the same esteem. And there are others, uncles and aunts mostly, who might produce that feeling but always less often, less intense, of shorter duration. It is as if my unconscious process—that enteric nervous system—measures the depth of my grief.

And so I am thankful, grateful, appreciative of my enteric nervous system, or of whatever it is that produces that unpleasant feeling. Were it to never occur when thinking of those most grieved I would wonder if I no longer treasured them.

Harvey Silverman

Three Poems

Scabs

From a distance, you cannot see the scars
How beautiful, you say
Soft brush strokes and blended lines
But your view is blurry
You do not see the creases
The scabs that ooze
How marvelous, you say
You do not see the inconsistencies
The rotting flesh below
The smell of burnt flesh only lingers so far

Smeared paint

From a distance, you cannot see
How beautiful, you say
Soft brush strokes and blended lines
But your view is blurred
You do not see the creases
The smeared paint from a heavy hand
How marvelous, you say
You do not see the inconsistencies
The discord of shades
How breathtaking, you say
From afar and up close
For much different reasons

Untitled

The world is on fucking fire
Zoom in, it's just pixels
Zoom out, it's a speck of dust

But right here, in this exact spot, you can see the
  flames rising

Meaghan Stout

Midbrain

(vision)(hearing)

01110010 01100001 01100100 01101001 01101111 00100000
01110011 01101001 01101100 01100101 01101110 01100011
01100101

My Eyes Have Seen the Impossible

I saw hope squatting in a rich man's eyes,
that was impossible two days ago;
then there was no hope lurking like a cloud
in the middle of the nervous sky,
not knowing how to leave the centre,
or linger longer in case someone must upload;
there was no smoke of war or inferno
rising from closed chimneys and skyscrapers;
no threat of the ground collapsing
to swallow the gazillions of smoke emitters;
there was just the scent of Jasmine
plodding over the surface of the street.
A tycoon huddled behind the gold steering
of his peerless, libertine limousine,
without pilfering a stare through the rear window
to watch me crouch on the asphalt of the road;
but he glued his eyes on the sweltering tar,
following every insect, every molten gold leaf
sprawling on the burnt road like a dead kidnapper.
Labyrinths of water climbed his body like tiny snakes,
blocking his view of the sunlight,
though darkness visits those born in the afternoon;
it's a delusion to keep still when violence
patrols like a thousand black daggers,
and things are no longer all they seem.

Jonathan Ukah

Pons

(unconscious)(processes)

01101101 01111001 01101111 01100011 01101100 01101111
01101110 01101001 01100011 00100000 01101010 01100101
01110010 01101011 01110011

Support, Please Hold

The grooming technician in Georgia is upset
that the timecard feature does not allow overnight punches.
I mention that the homeless rate for veterans
has tripled since the war in Iraq began a decade ago.

A business owner in Oregon complains
that his receipts aren't transferring into QuickBooks properly.
I tell him that a single mother in Maine was refused
coverage for her dead daughter's leukemia.

A store manager in Mississippi wants to know
why he can't charge customers on alternating Thursdays.
I relate a recent story about a CEO who was kicked to death
by a mob of unemployed factory workers in India.

With unwavering attitude, the cashier in Ontario declares
that the program does whatever it feels like.
I explain that we are superior to computers; they do not feel
or think, or assume, or judge, or need, or want.

They cannot make your employees smarter,
ask stupid questions about things beyond their control,
shake their fists at the sky or lay blame on others
for their own misfortunes and shortcomings.

A belligerent owner in Texas shouts obscenities
between lengthy tirades against the company.
He is unhappy with how the software functions.
He assures me he could do better himself.

I describe to him a tsunami in the south pacific
that battered a coastline, destroying houses and roads,
wiping out bloodlines, eradicating an entire culture
as if erasing words from a white board.

S. Michael Wilson

Medulla oblongata

(heartbeat)(breathing)

01101111 01101110 01100101 00100000 01100100 01100001
01111001 00100000 01101001 01110100 00100000 01110111
01101001 01101100 01101100 00100000 01100001 01101100
01101100 00100000 01110011 01110100 01101111 01110000

Theia to Earth*

I was just jamming, see, a teenage protoplanet,
fast but wobbly, spaced out. Clueless
when I, you know, crash-landed
right into your lap.

I was a junkyard kid, you had a double-wide.
I took your jumble for maturity, bulk
for worth. Took a bang for love.
Then you blew me off.

Not a smooth move, bigshot. Gases vaporized,
I'm still around, cooled into the moon
always pulling at you. Stuck
to your orbit. Plus

part of me sank in. Down where you don't look,
between crust and core, seismic waves
slow-dance. That's me. Gone?
Not in 4 billion years.

Kristin Camitta Zimet

* *Nature Briefing* newsletter, November 1, 2023, "Impact with a body called
Theia 4.5 billion years ago left remnants deep inside Earth—and also
created the Moon."

Spinal Cord

(support)(coordination)

01100110 01101001 01101110 01100100 00100000 01110101
01110011

Nerve Endings

(transduction)(transmission)

01110000 01101100 01100101 01100001 01110011 01100101

Contributors

Bill Beachly has retired from a long stint as a biology professor at Hastings College to the Smokey Hills of Kansas where he watches sunrise and sunset, tends critters and reads. His essays have appeared in *Prairie Fire* and *Nebraskaland*. This poem was inspired by a recent article in *Science*.

Ali Beheler (she/her) is a Virginia-born writer, professor, and doggie mama living in Nebraska. Her poems appear in *Harpur Palate*, *Tupelo Quarterly*, *ballast journal*, *Rogue Agent*, *Spoon River Poetry Review*, *Willows Wept Review*, *Up the Staircase Quarterly*, and elsewhere. Winner of the Milton J. Kessler Memorial Prize and the *SRPR* Editor's Prize, as well as an honorable mention in the Rash Poetry Awards, she teaches at Hastings College in Hastings, Nebraska. Find her at www.alibeheler.com.

Charlie Brice placed third in the 2021 Allen Ginsberg Poetry Prize. His ninth full-length poetry collection is *Tragedy in the Arugula Aisle* (Arroyo Seco Press, 2025). His poetry has been nominated three times for the Best of Net Anthology and the Pushcart Prize and has appeared in *Atlanta Review*, *The Honest Ulsterman*, *Ibbetson Street*, *Chiron Review*, *The MacGuffin*, and elsewhere.

Ulrick Casimir lives, writes, and teaches on the college/university level in the Pacific Northwest. Ulrick earned his BA from North Carolina State University and an MFA in Creative Writing from the University of North Carolina at Greensboro; he also holds an MA and a PhD, both in English, from the University of Oregon, where for the past several years he has taught writing and film for the English department and for Clark Honors College. Ulrick's scholarly work has appeared in the film journal *Jump Cut*, and his short fiction and poetry have appeared in *Plainsongs*. *Children of the Night*, published by Corpus Callosum Press in 2018, was his debut story collection.

Michael Catherwood's books are *Dare*, *If You Turned Around Quickly*, *Projector* from Stephen F. Austin Press, and *Near Misses* from WSC Press. He was former editor at The Backwaters Press and has been an associate editor at *Plainsongs* since 1995. Recent poems have appeared in *The Opiate*, *As It Ought to Be Magazine*, *Pennsylvania English*, *Zoetic Press*, and *Common Ground Review*. He's a cancer survivor, retired, and lives in Omaha, Nebraska, with his wife, Cindy.

Chad M. Christensen is the managing editor of the WSC Press and the director of the Plains Writers Series. He earned his MFA from the University of Nebraska Omaha and teaches writing and publishing at Wayne State College. His books of lo-fi poetry are *Ground Bound* and *Shoot from the Hip*.

Kevin Clouther is the author of the story collections *Maximum Speed* (Cornerstone) and *We Were Flying to Chicago* (Catapult). He is an Associate Professor at the University of Nebraska Omaha Writer's Workshop, where he directs the MFA in Writing. He lives with his wife and two children in Omaha.

Michael Detelj, 35, lives in Southington, Connecticut. A former touring musician, videographer, and visual artist, he has also been published in *The Talon Review*. Detelj describes himself as a therapy enthusiast, sober-curious hedonist, corporate sales rep, and Renaissance man with an extensive background as a singer/songwriter. He has not been involved with social media beyond LinkedIn since 2019.

Bart Edelman's poetry collections include *Crossing the Hackensack*, *Under Damaris' Dress*, *The Alphabet of Love*, *The Gentle Man*, *The Last Mojito*, *The Geographer's Wife*, *Whistling to Trick the Wind*, and *This Body Is Never at Rest: New and Selected Poems 1993–2023*. His work has been anthologized in textbooks published by City Lights Books, Harcourt Brace, Longman, and Prentice Hall. He lives in Pasadena, California.

Becky Faber, the author of *One Small Photo*, has had poems published in journals and anthologies, including *Nebraska Presence* (Backwaters Press). She received the 2024 Mari Sandoz Award and the 2021 Mildred Bennett Award for her contributions to Nebraska literature. Becky placed third in the 2024 Nebraska Poetry Society's open poetry contest.

Harrison Fisher has published twelve collections of poems, four of them book-length: *Blank Like Me*, *Curtains for You*, *UHFO*, and, most recently, *Poematics of the Hyperbloody Real*. In 2025, Fisher has new poems in *All Existing, Amsterdam Review, The Basilisk Tree, Chewers and Masticadores, eMerge, The Kleksograph, Misfitmagazine, Rat's Ass Review, Sheila-Na-Gig,* and *Trampoline.*

Valentine Freeman's work has been published in *The Believer, Weekday by Publication Studio, Portland Review, Livermore Street,* and elsewhere, and is forthcoming in the *Dopamine x Semiotext(e) Anthology 003.* Her chapbook *What's Truly is Feral* was selected by Marvin Bell for his New Poets Series. She lives in Los Osos, California, with her wife and animals.

Christopher Goedert sees himself as a temporary guest wandering around an incredible world full of natural wonder. He advocates for the health of that incredible world. He walks, runs, and hikes. He also draws and creates other forms of art.

Sarah Das Gupta is a poet from Cambridge, UK, whose work has been published in over twenty countries. She was recently nominated for the Best of the Net and a Dwarf Star.

Peycho Kanev is the author of 12 poetry collections and three chapbooks, published in the USA and Europe. His poems have appeared in many literary magazines, such as *Rattle, Poetry Quarterly, Evergreen Review, Front Porch Review, Hawaii Review, Barrow Street, Sheepshead Review, Off the Coast, The Adirondack Review, Sierra Nevada Review, The Cleveland Review,* and many others.

After a career in nonprofit health care, **Dennis Lum** volunteers with Legal Assistance for Seniors and on Ability Now Bay Area's Board of Directors, a community organization supporting adults with disabilities. He holds a Master of Public Health from UC Berkeley and has become an avid student of poetry. He studies, reads, and writes poetry with two poetry groups.

Margaret Marcum recently graduated from the MFA program in creative writing at Florida Atlantic University. Her poems have appeared in *Amethyst Review, NonBinary Review, Scapegoat Review, October Hill Magazine,* and *Children, Churches, and Daddies,* among others. She is also author of the poetry chapbook *Recognition of Movement* (Bottlecap Press, 2023).

Matt Mason served as Nebraska State Poet from 2019 to 2024 and has run poetry workshops in Botswana, Romania, Nepal, and Belarus for the State Department. His poetry has appeared in *The New York Times*, *Rattle*, *Poet Lore*, *Prairie Schooner*, and more. He's received a Pushcart Prize as well as a fellowship from the Academy of American Poets. Find more at https://matt.midverse.com/

Thomas Mixon has poems and stories in *Acta Victoriana*, *Eye to the Telescope*, *Apple Valley Review*, and elsewhere. He's trying to write a few books.

Maggie Rieckman grew up in a small town in Nebraska called Clay Center and is currently residing in Madrid, Spain. This duality of place often manifests in her poetry and art. Through the expression of her longing and sense of belonging, Maggie can feel at home, even when far away from the Great Plains.

Harvey Silverman is a retired old coot who writes nonfiction primarily for his own enjoyment.

Meaghan Stout is a writer, photographer, and "wannabe artist" with a BA in philosophy, religious studies, and international studies. She lives in Lincoln, Nebraska.

Jonathan Chibuike Ukah writes from London, England. His poems have been featured in many literary magazines and anthologies. He has won literary prizes and Pushcart nominations.

S. Michael Wilson (he/him) is a poet and author currently based out of Texas. He is the editor of the book *Monster Rally* and the author of the book *Performed by Lugosi*. His poetry, short fiction, and nonfiction have appeared in numerous anthologies and magazines, and he is the First Prize Winner of the 2016 Wergle Flomp Humor Poetry Contest.

Kristin Camitta Zimet is the author of *Take in My Arms the Dark* and coauthor of *A Tender Time*. Her poems are in a great many journals in eight countries and have been performed in concert halls, art galleries, and arboretums. She was the editor of *The Sow's Ear Poetry Review*.